food for
Lovers

food for
Lovers

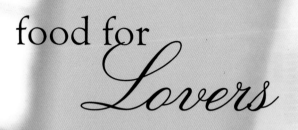

RYLAND
PETERS
& SMALL

LONDON NEW YORK

Designer Sarah Fraser

Commissioning Editor
      Elsa Petersen-Schepelern

Editor Sharon Cochrane

Picture Research Emily Westlake

Production Sheila Smith and
      Deborah Wehner

Art Director Gabriella Le Grazie

Publishing Director Alison Starling

Index Hilary Bird

First published in the United States in 2006
by Ryland Peters & Small, Inc.
519 Broadway, 5th Floor
New York, NY 10012
www.rylandpeters.com

10 9 8 7 6 5 4 3 2 1

Notes
All spoon measurements are level unless
otherwise specified.

All eggs are large unless otherwise
specified. Uncooked or partly cooked
eggs should not be served to the very
young, the very old, those with
compromised immune systems, or
to pregnant women.

Ovens should be preheated to the specified
temperature. If using a convection oven,
cooking times should be reduced according
to the manufacturer's instructions.

Library of Congress Cataloging-in-Publication Data

Food for lovers.
   p. cm.
  Includes index.
  ISBN-13: 978-1-84172-962-6
  ISBN-10: 1-84172-962-0
  1. Cookery.
  TX652.F5977 2006
  641.5--dc22
                       2005014299

Printed in China

Contents

Aphrodisiac Foods

For centuries many cultures have believed that certain foods possess aphrodisiac qualities—from the Aztecs who thought their highly prized chocolate enhanced sexual prowess, to the Romans who considered garlic capable of stimulating sexual desire.

Whether it's chocolate or oysters, asparagus or strawberries, aphrodisiac foods are a sure-fire way to revive any relationship. The recipes in this book are designed to set your desire alight, so if you think your relationship needs a boost, get cooking and bring the flames of passion to life.

Apricots *are a blushing fruit, considered to be a symbol of sensuality by the ancient Chinese*

Asparagus *is regarded by several cultures as a stimulant because of its erotic shape*

Bananas *have a suggestive shape, but also contain sex hormone-producing minerals*

Champagne *there's something in the bubbles*

Cherries *are very sensual, especially when dipped in melted chocolate*

Chocolate *legend says that the Aztec Emperor Montezuma drank 50 cups of frothy xocolatl before visiting his harem*

Eggs, *including caviar, stimulate the libido*

Figs *are erotic, fleshy fruits said to act as a powerful sexual stimulant*

Garlic *was considered an aphrodisiac by the Greeks, Egyptians, Romans, Chinese, and Japanese*

Ginger *stimulates the circulatory system and gets you "in the mood"*

Honey *is a derivation of the word "honeymoon," during which the couple would drink mead (honey wine)*

Licorice *is said to enhance love and lust, especially in women*

Nuts, *particularly pine nuts, have been used for centuries to make up love potions*

Oysters *Casanova was said to eat 50 of them each morning to enhance his sexual prowess*

Peaches *make a sensuous treat with their curvaceous shape and succulent texture*

Red meat *will give you the strength you need for a night of passion*

Rose petals *are the epitome of edible romance*

Saffron *is widely used as an aphrodisiac in Asia and the Middle East*

Seafood *is high in phosphorus, iodine, and often zinc, which increase sexual potency*

Strawberries *are regarded as a powerful stimulant—the perfect finger food for lovers*

Tomatoes *are known as the "love apple" in French—say no more…*

Breakfast in Bed

The way to a man's heart is through his stomach.
Fanny Fern (1811–1872)

Stirring a little creamy goat cheese into lightly scrambled eggs transforms a simple dish into something special enough to serve for breakfast in bed. The nasturtium flowers add a touch of romance as well as a delightful flash of color.

creamy eggs
with goat cheese

6 eggs

¼ cup light cream

1 tablespoon chopped fresh marjoram or thyme

2 tablespoons butter

3 oz. goat cheese, diced (about ¾ cup)

a small handful of nasturtium flowers, torn (optional)

sea salt and freshly ground black pepper

toasted walnut or whole-wheat bread, for serving

serves 2

Put the eggs, cream, marjoram or thyme, and a little salt and pepper in a bowl and beat well. Melt the butter in a nonstick saucepan, add the eggs, and stir over low heat until the eggs begin to set.

Stir in the goat cheese and continue to cook briefly, stirring all the time, until the cheese melts into the eggs. Add the nasturtium flowers, if using, and spoon onto the toast. Serve immediately.

Dunking toast into the perfect soft-boiled egg is one of the simple pleasures in life. Well, it's even better when you dip in asparagus spears—and it's much more sensual, too.

soft-boiled eggs
with asparagus

Tie the asparagus into 2 bunches of 6 with kitchen twine. Steam or boil it for 3 to 4 minutes until just tender. Drain and keep warm.

Meanwhile, gently lower the eggs into a saucepan of gently boiling water, cook for 4 minutes, then transfer them to egg cups. Remove the tops of the eggs with a knife and discard them. Sprinkle the eggs with salt and pepper to taste, then serve with the asparagus and some toast, if you like.

12 thick asparagus spears

4 eggs, at room temperature

sea salt and freshly ground black pepper

toast, for serving (optional)

serves 2

honey-roasted peaches
with ricotta and coffee-bean sugar

This is a mouthwatering recipe, to be enjoyed on a warm summer morning. Grinding whole coffee beans with a lump of sugar is typically Italian and adds a delicious crunch to the dish.

Put the peach or nectarine halves, cut side up, in the prepared ovenproof dish. Drizzle with the honey and roast in a preheated oven at 425°F for 15 to 20 minutes, until the fruit is tender and caramelized. Remove from the oven and let cool slightly.

Put the coffee beans and sugar in a coffee grinder and blitz very briefly, until the beans and sugar are coarsely ground.

Spoon the peaches or nectarines onto plates, top with a scoop of ricotta, sprinkle with the sugary coffee beans, then serve.

2 large peaches or nectarines, cut in half and pits removed

1 tablespoon honey

1 teaspoon coffee beans

1 teaspoon sugar

$^1/_2$ cup ricotta cheese, chilled

an ovenproof dish lined with parchment paper or foil

serves 2

sweet bruschetta *with figs*

1 tablespoon quince
paste*

1 tablespoon butter

1 tablespoon port

6 ripe figs, cut in half

2 slices of brioche loaf
or challah

confectioners' sugar,
for dusting

cinnamon, for dusting

yogurt, for serving

serves 2

Juicy fresh figs are a sweet—and
sexy—breakfast treat. Quince is
also a food for lovers.

Put the quince paste, butter, and port in a small
saucepan and heat gently until melted. Put the
figs, cut side up, in an ovenproof dish. Spoon
the port mixture over them, making sure the
surface of each fig is well covered. Cook the
figs under a preheated hot broiler for 3 to
5 minutes, until the figs are caramelized and
heated through.

Meanwhile, toast the brioche or challah
on a stovetop grill pan. Transfer to heated
serving plates and sprinkle immediately with
confectioners' sugar and cinnamon. Put the
figs on top and serve with a spoonful of yogurt.

*Note Quince paste is available from gourmet
stores. If you can't find it, use red currant jelly
or raspberry preserve instead.

red berry sauce

about 1 1/2 lb. strawberries

1 tablespoon freshly squeezed lemon juice

1/4 cup sugar

waffle batter

1 2/3 cups all-purpose flour

1/4 teaspoon salt

1 1/2 teaspoons baking powder

2 eggs, separated

1 tablespoon butter, melted

1 cup milk

for serving

2 cups strawberry ice cream

confectioners' sugar, for dusting

an electric 4-heart-patterned waffle iron, greased

a heart-shaped cookie cutter

serves 4

These heart-shaped waffles make a deliciously romantic start to the day.

waffle hearts

To make the red berry sauce, put the strawberries, lemon juice, and sugar in a saucepan and heat gently until the juices run. When the berries have become pale and the juice dark, push them through a plastic strainer. Set aside.

To make the waffle batter, sift the flour, salt, and baking powder into a bowl and make a well in the center. Beat the egg yolks until creamy. Beat the egg whites in a second bowl until stiff and frothy. Pour the melted butter into the flour, then the egg yolks and milk. Mix well, then fold in the beaten egg whites.

Heat the waffle iron until faintly smoking. Pour a little batter into each compartment and spread it over quickly. Close the waffle iron and leave for 1 minute until golden brown. Transfer the waffle to a heated plate and cook the remaining waffles in the same way. Break the waffles into the heart segments.

Using the cookie cutter, make 4 strawberry ice cream hearts, 1 1/2 inches thick. Put a waffle heart on each of 4 chilled plates, top with an ice cream heart, then a second waffle heart. Drizzle each portion with 1 tablespoon strawberry sauce, dust with confectioners' sugar, and serve.

Romantic Dinners

Whosoever says truffle, utters a grand word, which awakens erotic
and gastronomic ideas…
Jean-Anthelme Brillat-Savarin (1755–1826)

The truffle oil is an optional luxury but it is wonderful with egg and asparagus, and it will help boost the passion levels, too. Truffles were much prized by the Romans for their erotic powers, so do use the oil if you can.

asparagus *with egg and truffle butter*

2 cage-free eggs

3 tablespoons unsalted butter, softened

a little truffle oil (optional)

1/2 lb. fresh asparagus, trimmed

sea salt and freshly ground black pepper

serves 2

Hard-boil the eggs for about 10 minutes, depending upon their size. Let cool in cold water, then peel them. Cut the eggs in half and remove the yolks. Finely chop the whites and set aside. Mash the yolks with the butter until well blended. Add a drop or two of truffle oil, if using, and season with salt. Cover and keep at room temperature.

Steam the asparagus for about 12 minutes until tender. Divide it between 2 warm plates, sprinkle with chopped egg white and salt and pepper, then serve with the golden butter. (The butter can be either spooned on top to melt into the spears or served separately in little dishes to spread onto each mouthful.)

Oysters are the ultimate aphrodisiac. Purists would never serve their oysters any way but naked (the oysters, that is), but the Thai dressing adds some spice.

fresh oysters *with thai dressing*

To make the dressing, put the lemongrass, lime leaf, fish sauce, lime juice, mirin, and sugar in a blender, then add 1 tablespoon water. Blend well, then set aside to infuse for 2 hours. Strain into a clean bowl and stir in the cucumber and cilantro.

To shuck the oysters, put them cupped side down on a flat counter. Insert a knife into the hinge and twist it until the top shell is loosened, then twist it off, reserving as much of the oyster liquor as possible. Spoon the dressing over the oysters and serve at once on a bed of ice.

12 fresh oysters

ice cubes, for serving

thai dressing

1 stalk of lemongrass, very thinly sliced

1 kaffir lime leaf, very thinly sliced, or the finely grated zest of $^1/_2$ lime

1 tablespoon Thai fish sauce

$^3/_4$ tablespoon freshly squeezed lime juice

$^3/_4$ tablespoon mirin (sweetened Japanese rice wine)

$^1/_2$ teaspoon sugar

$1^1/_4$-inch piece of cucumber, peeled and cut into small cubes

a few cilantro leaves

serves 2

rack of lamb

1 rack of lamb

2 cups baby spinach, about
$\frac{1}{2}$ lb., wilted

marinating syrup

1 tablespoon cranberry sauce

$\frac{1}{4}$ cup sweet sherry

$\frac{1}{4}$ cup sherry vinegar
(if unavailable, use
red wine vinegar)

$1\frac{1}{2}$ tablespoons sugar

1 tablespoon soy sauce

1 sprig of rosemary

1 small garlic clove, sliced

gravy

$1\frac{1}{2}$–2 tablespoons
unsalted butter

$\frac{1}{4}$ cup white vermouth

$\frac{1}{2}$ cup lamb or chicken broth

sea salt and freshly ground
black pepper

nonstick parchment paper
or aluminum foil

a roasting pan

serves 2

To make the marinating syrup, put the cranberry sauce in a saucepan, add the sherry, vinegar, sugar, soy sauce, rosemary, and 2 slices of the garlic, and boil to reduce and form a syrup. Brush the syrup all over the rack of lamb and put it in a plastic bag along with the rest of the syrup. Set aside to marinate for 2 hours, turning every 30 minutes.

When ready to cook, wipe the excess marinade off the rack of lamb (reserving the marinade), set it on nonstick parchment paper or a sheet of foil in a roasting pan, and roast in a preheated oven at 500°F for 8 minutes. Remove from the oven and let rest in a warm place for up to 2 hours.

To serve, reheat the rack for 6 to 8 minutes in the very hot oven, then slice it between the bones. Put a bed of cooked spinach on each plate, then put the cutlets on top, crossing over the bones.

Meanwhile, to make the gravy, put the butter in a small saucepan, add the vermouth, and boil until reduced by half. Add the broth and 1 to 2 teaspoons of the leftover marinade, bring to a boil, and let it reduce again to improve the flavor. Season to taste with salt and pepper. Pour the gravy around the meat, then serve immediately.

½ lb. potatoes (suitable for baking and frying), peeled and cut into ¼-inch slices

safflower oil for deep-frying, plus ½ tablespoon for grilling

2 sirloin or rib eye steaks, about 10 oz. each, 1 inch thick

sea salt and freshly ground black pepper

shallot butter

½ stick unsalted butter, softened

1 shallot, finely chopped

⅓ cup red wine

a large sprig of tarragon

several sprigs of flat-leaf parsley

½ teaspoon coarse sea salt

¼ teaspoon coarsely ground black pepper

a large pan with frying basket, or an electric deep-fryer

serves 2

steak and fries

To make the shallot butter, melt half of the butter very gently in a saucepan. Add the shallot and cook until softened. Add the wine, bring to a boil, and cook until syrupy and the wine has almost completely evaporated. Let cool. Put the cooled shallot, remaining butter, tarragon, parsley, salt, and pepper in a small food processor and blend briefly. Transfer to a piece of waxed paper and roll up into a log shape. Chill until firm.

To prepare the fries, cut the potato slices into ¼-inch strips. Put them in a bowl of ice water for at least 5 minutes. Drain and pat dry. Fill a large pan one-third full with the oil or, if using a deep-fryer, to the manufacturer's recommended level. Heat the oil to 375°F or until a cube of bread will brown in 30 seconds. Working in batches, put 2 large handfuls of potato strips into the frying basket, lower into the oil, and fry for about 4 minutes. Remove and drain on paper towels. Repeat with the remaining strips. Reheat the oil to 375°F, then fry the strips for a second time until crisp and golden, about 2 minutes. Drain on paper towels, sprinkle with salt, and keep warm.

Rub the steaks on both sides with the oil. Heat a ridged stove-top grill pan, add the steaks, and cook for 1½ to 2 minutes on each side for a rare steak, or for 3½ to 4 minutes on each side for medium-rare. Remove from the pan and season both sides. Let stand for a few minutes, then serve with the butter and fries.

panna cotta *with rose-petal syrup*

1 tablespoon gelatin granules

²/₃ cup light cream

1 vanilla bean, split lengthwise, seeds removed

¹/₃ cup sugar

1 lb. mascarpone cheese (about 2 cups)

¹/₂ teaspoon pure almond extract or 1 tablespoon amaretto liqueur

1 teaspoon rose water

syrup

2 tablespoons vanilla sugar

¹/₂ cup white wine

for serving

petals of 1 scented rose

6–8 cantucci or amaretti cookies (optional)

6–8 small pots, cups, or dishes, ¹/₂ cup each, oiled

serves 6–8

Put the gelatin in a heatproof bowl, add ¹/₄ cup water, and let it swell.

Put the cream, vanilla bean, and its seeds in a small saucepan, heat to simmering, then almost to boiling, then turn off the heat. Let stand for 2 minutes. Stir in the soaked gelatin until it dissolves. Remove the vanilla bean (you can dry it and use it to perfume a jar of sugar, if liked).

Put the sugar, mascarpone, almond extract or amaretto liqueur, and ¹/₂ teaspoon of the rose water in a bowl and beat until creamy and smooth. Whisk in the gelatin mixture, then pour into the prepared pots, cups, or dishes, and chill for at least 2 hours.

Meanwhile, to make the syrup, put the vanilla sugar and white wine in a small saucepan, heat over low heat and stir until dissolved and bubbling. Let cool slightly, then stir in the remaining rose water.

Serve the panna cotta in their pots, or turned out, with a trickle of syrup and several scented rose petals, and crisp cookies such as cantucci or amaretti.

rose petal tart

12 oz. frozen puff pastry dough, thawed

1/2 cup plain yogurt

1 1/2 cups heavy cream

1 large egg yolk

2-3 tablespoons rose water

2 tablespoons sugar

crystallized rose petals

1 egg white

petals of 2-4 scented roses

superfine sugar

a wire rack or waxed paper

a heart-shaped or round tart pan, 10 inches diameter

foil and baking beans

makes a 10-inch tart

To crystallize the rose petals, put the egg white in a bowl, beat until frothy, then paint it onto clean dry petals. Sprinkle with sugar to coat completely, then arrange on a wire rack or waxed paper and leave in a warm place to dry out and crisp—at least overnight. Let cool, but do not put them in the refrigerator. Store between layers of paper towels in an airtight container.

Roll out the dough as thinly as possible and line the tart pan with it, trimming to leave 1/8 inch hanging over the edge. Turn this inwards to make a rim. Prick the bottom with a fork, then chill or freeze for 15 minutes. Line with foil and baking beans and bake blind in a preheated oven at 450°F for 12 to 15 minutes. Turn the oven down to 400°F, remove the foil and beans, and return the pie crust to the oven for 5 minutes to dry out. You may have to flatten the pastry if it puffs up.

Turn the oven down to 350°F. Put the yogurt, 1/4 cup of the cream, the egg yolk, rose water, and sugar in a bowl and mix well. Put the remaining cream in a bowl and beat until soft peaks form, then fold into the yogurt mixture. Spoon into the baked pie crust, level the surface, and bake for about 20 minutes. It will seem almost runny, but will set as it cools. Cover and chill until firm. Decorate with the crystallized rose petals. Serve slightly cold.

Cozy Suppers

Men become passionately attached to women who
know how to cosset them with delicate tidbits.
Honoré de Balzac (1799–1859)

This is a hands-on dish that's perfect for an intimate supper for two. Serve these shrimp with lots of fresh, crusty bread to mop up the garlicky sauce.

garlic shrimp

¼ cup olive oil

1 lb. shrimp tails, with shells

4–5 garlic cloves, chopped

a handful of flat-leaf parsley, chopped

coarse sea salt and freshly ground black pepper

1 lemon, cut into wedges, for serving

serves 2

Heat the oil in a large sauté pan or skillet. When hot but not smoking, add the shrimp and garlic and cook for 3 to 5 minutes until the shrimp turn pink. Be careful not to let the garlic burn. Remove the pan from the heat, sprinkle the shrimp with salt, pepper, and parsley, and mix well. Serve immediately, with lemon wedges.

asparagus risotto

Put the hot broth in a wide pan. Add the asparagus and boil for about 6 minutes until tender. Drain the broth into a regular saucepan and simmer gently. Plunge the asparagus into cold water, then drain and cut into small pieces.

To poach the eggs, fill a saucepan with cold water and bring to a boil. Add the vinegar, then give it a good stir to create a whirlpool. Slip an egg into the vortex, then simmer very gently for 2 to 3 minutes. Using a slotted spoon, transfer the poached egg to a pan of warm water. Repeat with the other eggs. Keep them warm while you make the risotto.

Melt half the butter in a large, heavy saucepan and add the shallots. Cook gently for 5 to 6 minutes until soft, golden, and translucent but not browned. Add the rice and stir until well coated with the butter and heated through. Begin adding the hot broth, a large ladle at a time, stirring gently until each ladle has almost been absorbed by the rice. The risotto should be kept at a bare simmer throughout cooking, so don't let the rice dry out—add more broth as necessary. Continue until the rice is tender and creamy, but the grains still firm, 15 to 20 minutes.

Taste, season with salt and pepper, then beat in the Parmesan and the remaining butter. Fold in the drained asparagus. Cover, let rest for a few minutes, then serve topped with a drained poached egg, the parsley and tarragon, and Parmesan shavings.

about 6 cups hot vegetable or chicken broth

1 lb. fresh green or purple-tipped asparagus, trimmed

1 teaspoon tarragon or white wine vinegar

6 fresh eggs, each cracked into separate cups

1 stick unsalted butter

2 shallots, finely chopped (or 2 tablespoons chopped mild onion)

2 1/3 cups risotto rice, preferably carnaroli

1/2 cup freshly grated Parmesan cheese

sea salt and freshly ground black pepper

for serving

1 tablespoon chopped fresh parsley and tarragon, mixed

Parmesan cheese shavings

serves 6

This is easy to make and ideal for a cozy supper, since it should be made one day in advance. You should use good-quality chocolate, but anything over 70 percent cocoa solids will be too much.

chocolate mousse

7 oz. dark chocolate
(70 percent cocoa solids),
broken into pieces
(about 1¼ cups)

2 tablespoons unsalted
butter, cut into small pieces

1 vanilla bean, split
lengthwise

3 eggs, separated

a pinch of salt

2 tablespoons sugar

whipped cream, for serving
(optional)

serves 4

Put the chocolate in a heatproof glass bowl and melt it in the microwave on High for 40 seconds. Remove, stir, and repeat until almost completely melted. Remove, then stir in the butter. Using the tip of a small sharp knife, scrape the seeds from the vanilla bean into the chocolate. Add the egg yolks, stir, and set aside.

Put the egg whites and salt in a large, greasefree bowl and, using an electric mixer, beat until foaming. Continue beating and add the sugar. Beat on high until the mixture is glossy and firm.

Carefully fold the whites into the chocolate with a rubber spatula until no more white specks can be seen.

Transfer the mousse to serving dishes and refrigerate for at least 6 hours, preferably overnight. Serve with whipped cream, if you like.

strawberries, meringue, and mascarpone cream

1/2 lb. strawberries (about 2 cups)

freshly squeezed juice of 1/2 orange

2–3 tablespoons sugar

1 teaspoon grated unwaxed orange zest

4 oz. mascarpone cheese (about 1/2 cup)

1/2 cup heavy cream

4 ready-made meringue nests

fresh mint leaves, for serving

serves 2

Any shape of meringue can be used here, and chocolate meringues are good, too. This is also very pretty served in tall, thin glasses, with the meringue (perhaps broken into pieces), cream, and fruit built up in layers.

Wash the strawberries and pat them dry, then hull, trim (cut in half if large), and put in a bowl. Squeeze the orange juice over them. Add 1 to 1 1/2 tablespoons sugar to taste, and the orange zest. Stir gently until well blended, then set aside for at least 30 minutes or up to 6 hours.

Put the mascarpone in a bowl, then add the cream and 1 to 1 1/2 tablespoons sugar to taste. Beat well, then cover and refrigerate until needed.

When ready to serve, put 1 meringue nest on each plate. Top with half the mascarpone cream mixture, then add half the strawberries. Put the remaining meringue nests on top, add the mint leaves, and serve.

The best-quality chocolate, a hint of vanilla, lots of frothy milk topped with whipped cream, and grated chocolate—this is the ultimate hot drink for lovers.

the finest hot chocolate

3 oz. dark chocolate, broken into pieces (about ½ cup)

1 tablespoon sugar, or to taste

1 vanilla bean, split lengthwise

1¼ cups milk

⅓ cup heavy cream or whipping cream, whipped

freshly grated chocolate or unsweetened cocoa powder, for sprinkling

2 mugs, warmed

serves 2

Put the chocolate pieces, sugar, vanilla bean, and milk in a small, heavy saucepan. Heat gently, stirring, until the chocolate has melted, then bring to a boil, beating constantly with a balloon whisk, until very smooth and frothy. Remove the vanilla bean.

Pour the hot chocolate into warmed mugs, top with whipped cream and a sprinkling of freshly grated chocolate or cocoa powder, and serve immediately.

Little Treats

All mankind love a lover.
Ralph Waldo Emerson (1803–1882)

strawberries
and cherries *in chocolate*

1½ cups strawberries,
stems on

1½ cups cherries, stems on

1 oz. milk chocolate, broken
into small pieces (about
3 tablespoons)

1 oz. white chocolate,
broken into small pieces
(about 3 tablespoons)

1 oz. dark chocolate,
broken into small pieces
(about 3 tablespoons)

waxed paper

mini paper muffin cups
(optional)

serves 4

Divide the strawberries and cherries into 3 equal piles.

Put the milk, white, and dark chocolate in 3 separate cups
or mugs. Put the mugs in the top of a double boiler set
over steaming but not boiling water and melt the chocolate
gently. Do not let the bottom of the top pan touch the
water or let any water touch the chocolate, or the
chocolate will "seize" and be unusable.

Take a pile of the strawberries and a pile of the cherries,
dip them halfway into the melted milk chocolate, leaving
the tops and stems uncoated and visible. Lay the fruit on
a sheet of waxed paper and let set.

Take another pile each of the strawberries and cherries and
dip those into the white chocolate in the same way. Dip the
remaining fruit into the dark chocolate. Chill the coated
fruit for at least 1 hour.

To serve, peel off the waxed paper and put a selection of
fruit in a mini paper muffin cup. Alternatively, pile the fruit
onto a large serving plate and help yourselves.

Make one of these and serve it with two spoons. Containing chocolate, banana, nuts, and cherries, this sundae is sure to take your love life to new heights!

banana split

To make the chocolate sauce, heat the cream and sugar in a saucepan, then stir into the melted chocolate and mix well. Set aside.

To make the butterscotch sauce, put the sugar, cream, and butter in a saucepan and stir over medium heat until melted and boiling. Reduce the heat and simmer for 3 minutes. Set aside.

Put the banana halves in the long, shallow, glass dish. Put 3 scoops of ice cream down the length of the dish, between the 2 halves of banana. Drizzle 1 tablespoon each of the red berry sauce, chocolate sauce, and butterscotch sauce over the top. Spoon the whipped cream around the base of the dish and over the ice cream. Sprinkle with chopped nuts and top with the cherries. If using wafer cookies, set them in the ice cream at a jaunty angle.

1 ripe banana, sliced lengthwise

3 scoops of ice cream, one each of vanilla, chocolate, and strawberry

1 tablespoon Red Berry Sauce (see page 20)

2–4 tablespoons whipped cream

1 tablespoon crushed mixed nuts

2–3 maraschino cherries

2 wafer cookies, for serving (optional)

chocolate sauce

1 cup heavy cream

$1/4$ cup sugar

about 6 oz. dark chocolate, broken into pieces, melted (see page 51)

butterscotch sauce

$1/2$ cup brown sugar

$1/2$ cup heavy cream

$1/3$ cup butter

a long, shallow glass dish

makes 1, enough for 2 to share

Succulent, juicy strawberries are the perfect summertime treat. Peach slices can be substituted for the strawberries, if you prefer.

sugared strawberries

2 pints strawberries,
at room temperature

freshly squeezed juice of
1 lemon

3-5 tablespoons sugar

crème fraîche or
whipped cream,
for serving

serves 4–6

Trim the strawberries and put them in a pretty bowl. Add the lemon juice and 3 tablespoons sugar. Mix gently but thoroughly and let stand for about 15 minutes. Taste, and add more sugar if necessary.

This dish improves with standing, but don't leave it too long—about 1 hour is fine.

If using crème fraîche, sweeten it with 1 teaspoon sugar. Otherwise serve with whipped cream.

coffee and walnut kisses

These "kisses" are delicate walnut and coffee cookies sandwiched together with a rich chocolate-coffee ganache.

1 stick unsalted butter

4 1/2 tablespoons sugar

1/2 beaten egg

3/4 cup self-rising flour, sifted

1 teaspoon instant espresso powder

1/3 cup walnuts, finely chopped

ganache

4 oz. semisweet chocolate, broken into pieces

4 tablespoons unsalted butter

1/2 cup heavy cream

1 1/2 teaspoons instant espresso powder

2 cookie sheets covered with nonstick parchment paper

makes 12 "kisses"

Put the butter and sugar in a bowl and beat until creamy. Stir in the beaten egg, then fold in the sifted flour. Stir in the espresso powder, then the chopped walnuts. Put an even number of tablespoons of the mixture (about 24) onto the prepared cookie sheets, allowing room for them to spread. Bake in a preheated oven at 350°F for about 10 minutes, or until light brown around the edges. Remove from the oven, let cool and firm up on the tray for a couple of minutes, then carefully transfer to a wire rack and let them cool completely.

Meanwhile, to make the ganache, put the chocolate, butter, and cream in a saucepan and heat gently until the butter melts—do not let the mixture boil. Beat in the espresso powder. Remove the pan from the heat and stir with a wooden spoon. The mixture will thicken as it cools. Carefully sandwich the cool, fragile cookies together with the ganache. Store in an airtight container for up to 3 days.

bellini

Peaches galore, topped up with champagne—this classic cocktail makes a wonderful tipple for lovers.

¼ fresh peach, skinned

1 tablespoon crème de peche

a dash of peach bitters (optional)

champagne, to top up

peach ball, for garnishing

makes 1

Put the peach in a blender and blend to a purée. Transfer the purée to a champagne flute. Pour in the crème de peche and the peach bitters, if using, and gently top up with champagne, stirring carefully and continuously. Add a peach ball to the glass, then serve immediately.

This delicate cocktail combines ginger with champagne to delicious effect.

ginger champagne

2 thin slices of fresh ginger root

1 oz. vodka

champagne, to top up

makes 1

Put the ginger in a shaker and press with a barspoon or muddler to release the flavor. Add some ice and the vodka, shake well, and strain into a champagne flute. Top up with champagne and serve immediately.

strawberry cosmopolitan

"Muddle" the ripe strawberries in a cocktail shaker using a barspoon, add the remaining ingredients, and shake sharply. Strain into a frosted martini glass and garnish with ½ strawberry. Serve immediately.

3½ fresh strawberries, plus ½ for garnishing

1 oz. citrus vodka

¾ oz. Cointreau

1 tablespoon freshly squeezed lime juice

a dash of cranberry juice (optional)

makes 1

1¼ oz. lemon vodka

1 tablespoon freshly squeezed lime juice

1 tablespoon Cointreau

1¾ oz. cranberry juice

champagne, to float

orange zest, for garnishing (optional)

makes 1

cosmo royale

Put all the ingredients, except the champagne, in a cocktail shaker filled with ice. Shake sharply and strain into a frosted martini glass. Float the champagne on the surface and garnish with orange zest, if you like. Serve immediately.

Conversion Charts

Weights and measures have been rounded up
or down slightly to make measuring easier.

Volume equivalents:

American	Metric	Imperial
1 teaspoon	5 ml	
1 tablespoon	15 ml	
¼ cup	60 ml	2 fl.oz.
⅓ cup	75 ml	2½ fl.oz.
½ cup	125 ml	4 fl.oz.
⅔ cup	150 ml	5 fl.oz. (¼ pint)
¾ cup	175 ml	6 fl.oz.
1 cup	250 ml	8 fl.oz.

Weight equivalents:

Imperial	Metric
1 oz.	25 g
2 oz.	50 g
3 oz.	75 g
4 oz.	125 g
5 oz.	150 g
6 oz.	175 g
7 oz.	200 g
8 oz. (½ lb.)	250 g
9 oz.	275 g
10 oz.	300 g
11 oz.	325 g
12 oz.	375 g
13 oz.	400 g
14 oz.	425 g
15 oz.	475 g
16 oz. (1 lb.)	500 g
2 lb.	1 kg

Oven temperatures:

110°C	(225°F)	Gas ¼
120°C	(250°F)	Gas ½
140°C	(275°F)	Gas 1
150°C	(300°F)	Gas 2
160°C	(325°F)	Gas 3
180°C	(350°F)	Gas 4
190°C	(375°F)	Gas 5
200°C	(400°F)	Gas 6
220°C	(425°F)	Gas 7
230°C	(450°F)	Gas 8
240°C	(475°F)	Gas 9

Measurements:

Inches	Cm
¼ inch	5 mm
½ inch	1 cm
¾ inch	1.5 cm
1 inch	2.5 cm
2 inches	5 cm
3 inches	7 cm
4 inches	10 cm
5 inches	12 cm
6 inches	15 cm
7 inches	18 cm
8 inches	20 cm
9 inches	23 cm
10 inches	25 cm
11 inches	28 cm
12 inches	30 cm

Index

Credits

Key: a=above, b=below, r=right, l=left, c=center

Recipes

Maxine Clark: *pages 25, 34, 41*
Linda Collister: *page 46*
Hattie Ellis: *page 56*
Clare Ferguson: *page 33*
Jane Noraika: *page 51*
Elsa Petersen-Schepelern: *pages 20, 52*
Louise Pickford: *pages 12, 15, 16, 18, 26*
Ben Reed: *pages 59, 60*
Sonia Stevenson: *page 29*
Laura Washburn: *pages 30, 38, 42, 45, 55*

Photographs

Martin Brigdale: *7al, 24, 28–35, 39–43, 47, 54, 63*
David Brittain: *36, 49, 64 background*
Peter Cassidy: *4–5, 10, 12*
Dan Duchars: *48*
Daniel Farmer: *11*
Tom Leighton: *endpapers*
William Lingwood: *50–51, 58–61*
David Loftus: *64c inset*
James Merrell: *7bl*
David Montgomery: *8l inset, 64l inset*
David Munns: *2–3, 44*
Noel Murphy: *64r inset*
Debi Treloar: *1, 20–23, 53, 57*
Ian Wallace: *13–18, 27*
Polly Wreford: *37*
Francesca Yorke: *6, 7ar & br, 8–9*